Glimpses
of
God

Glimpses
of
God

Michelle J. Peele

Pentland Press, Inc.
www.pentlandpressusa.com

PUBLISHED BY PENTLAND PRESS, INC.
5122 Bur Oak Circle, Raleigh, North Carolina 27612
United States of America
919-782-0281

ISBN 1-57197-248-X
Library of Congress Control Number: 00-134884

Printed in the United States of America

Cover Photograph by Meredith Perdue

This is an account of a metamorphic journey. It is one that started in pain and travels through hope. This never-ending saga is shadowed with sorrow, but sprinkled with real-life glimpses of God. The persons and events are real. Let it help you.

Dear Michelle,

A thunderstorm rolls across the high plains, billowing and blowing as it charges forward. Some see it coming and are fearful. Others get caught inside the storm, with no preparation, and are overcome by the unknown.

But all who withstand the tempest are filled with relief and a determination to see what has protected them. Surrounding them is the light of a rainbow, light that has been waiting patiently to reveal itself. In a fleeting moment the survivors feel the peace offered by a glimpse of the light, a Glimpse of God.

I Love You,
Ed, your husband

This book is dedicated to my family. Without their everlasting love and support I would not have been able to complete this. They have all suffered the pain and the changes in me. Thank you!

FOREWORD

My mother's journey would indeed be a difficult one. I remember worrying about her constantly following Morgan's death. I recall waking up every morning to find her deeply involved in any book regarding death or grief. There were new books daily. She was searching for answers and insight, anything that would provide comfort while making her feel closer to Morgan.

Eventually she would grasp some words, a phrase, maybe a poem that would help. You can imagine my surprise and joy when the message my Mom grasped was not from any doctor, therapist, or writer, but the unspoken and unwritten signs of God that humans encounter every day.

MacKenzie Rowan

This is a story about pain. This is a story about grief. This is a story about a mother's greatest fear—the unexpected death of a child. It is almost unimaginable that woven into the tapestry of the unendurable pain is a true story of hope, faith and real glimpses of God.

I am recording this chronology of events in hopes that someday someone will read this in their own time of pain and start listening, seeing, and feeling God's attention to detail. With God there is no chaos. His plan is forever reaching and all encompassing. The glimpses of God that you are about to read are true. I did not realize their gift value until after the fact. They are not embellished or exaggerated, but from the heart. They are for your encouragement, growth, and education into the awesome power of our God.

I wasn't a stranger to God. At the same time, even though God smiled on me in many ways and I thanked Him often, I knew very little about the scriptures or about the people described in the Bible and their sufferings throughout time. I never felt comfortable speaking of God and His graces for fear of alienating people. My energy, my enthusiasm, my love of people and life would speak loudly enough of God's goodness. Mostly, because I had not had a very complete Christian upbringing, I felt educationally inferior where the Bible was concerned.

I had always been confused and intimidated by the mere language in the Bible. I knew the value of the Ten Commandments. I knew I was human and full of sin and that God would forgive

my slipping and losing sight of
His word. Knowing these basics
seemed to be enough, so I did not
look any deeper. I know now that
I am not alone. I believe the
majority of people find themselves
in this "gray zone" just as I did.
"Gray zone" is my term for people
who go to church and help out in
the congregation and in the
community. They are the majority
who "talk" the faith and even
think they are walking the faith,
but have never challenged
themselves nor had any
experience really challenge their
faith. I believe they are like I was
and they know very little about
the lessons of the Bible. Acting on
my knowledge of right from
wrong, working hard every day to
always be a better person should
have been enough to hold up my
end of the deal and I would earn
more of God's smiles and gifts.

Then March 5, 1999, came. It is a trite statement to say that my life was changed forever. As I write this in the everyday language that all can read and relate to, I realize that my life changed in two ways.

First, I would carry forever a hurt that actually made my heart and head ache. A hurt that punched at my very core and brought me to my knees.

Second, I would see how close God is to all of His children when they hurt. God is nearest to those who are suffering. God knew His plan would cause pain. God hurt with me on the night of March 5. God did His best to prepare me for the pain, but I didn't know that until many days later.

October 1998–March 1999

Building our own home
and literally doing all of the
finish construction ourselves
was difficult. Both my
husband, Ed, and I worked
full-time at our jobs and at the
house. I was a candidate for
Salesperson of the Year 1998,
having grown my territory and
client base by more than 50
percent over the previous year.
Morgan, the middle of my
three daughters, was going at a
pace that rivaled me. Along
with being an energetic, busy
senior at Pinecrest High
School, she was determined to
move her horse, Irish, here
from Ohio. Morgan spent her
summers working with a 4-H
group in Ohio, raising a steer
and riding and enjoying her
horse. She had set a goal for
herself to have Irish moved

down here to North Carolina in her senior year. It was her responsibility to handle every detail of the move and make all the arrangements for boarding Irish once he got here. To do that, she had to work two jobs every month except December, when she added a third position as a gift wrapper at Belk's Department Store. Morgan was dedicated to the task at hand. All of this was in order to buy the needed tack and pay for board, shots, and general upkeep on her beloved horse.

Meredith, our youngest, also kept us all busy with school projects and attending her sports events. Along with that hectic pace, all the girls were required to clean the construction site on occasion and keep their grades up.

Morgan also took a jewelry design class at Meredith College, one and a half hours away, one night a week in preparation for her upcoming graduation. In the fall she planned to put her formidable artistic talents to use by entering a jewelry design school in San Francisco.

We all survived a hectic holiday season. Our attention was focused on maintaining the normal demands and to continue work on our long-awaited home. MacKenzie, our oldest daughter, and her friend Noah came home from Germany for the holidays. We all thought we were captains of our own ships and doing an awesome job of working and juggling. Hooray for us!

Mid-February came and found Morgan fully immersed in her senior journalism project. Thank God that despite the fact that we were so busy, we still had family meals together.

Family life in 1999 was different for us compared to many of the families we knew. We noticed it more and more as we listened to other kids and their parents comment on their own daily routines. We are a blended family. I raised three girls alone for seven years, and we were very dependent on each other. Our dysfunction was being too dependent, loving too much, doing everything together and talking about everything. When I married Ed in 1997, he brought twin daughters with him into the

relationship. The twins came to stay with us every Wednesday and every other weekend, which added to the confusion and fun. He was totally amazed and sometimes shocked at the conversations around our dinner table. Everyone attended dinner together. Always.

There seemed to be constant activity at our home throughout the years. Parties, impromptu get-togethers, lots of song, dance, and laughter. Of course, arguments, too. When you put four energetic and enthusiastic women together and add two more and the dreaded male, typical fights break out. Our household could have been best described as a combination of *Brady Bunch* and *The Munsters*.

During one of those meals, Morgan commented on one of the front-page stories in the local paper. Two high school girls from a neighboring community had been killed in a tragic auto accident. We discussed the absolute horror of the accident. Morgan stated that if she were ever killed in an accident that she would want her organs donated and want to be cremated. The subjects were discussed heavily. I remember saying,

"That's enough, I agree, and let's not talk about it anymore. It gives me the creeps."

The conversation seemed ominous and I felt that if we talked about it any more it would come true. I wanted to knock on wood at that moment. If we spent any more time

discussing the unimaginable
pain of those events then it
might possibly happen to us.

*Glimpse of God: He tried to
prepare me. He helped me know
Morgan's wishes because He knew
what was lying ahead. God gave
me the answers in advance to the
upcoming questions.*

MacKenzie had been
selected to travel with an
international education
program called Up With
People. She had been chosen to
hold the lead in an original
musical performance. Her cast
of over 200 students performed
all over the world to help build
understanding and cooperation
among people of different
backgrounds. MacKenzie had
been traveling with the cast all

over Europe. She had an opportunity to come back to North Carolina to perform on February 24. The entire family and numerous friends made a three-hour trip to Henderson, North Carolina, to see her perform. It was the only time Morgan had the opportunity to see her sister on stage with this esteemed group. It was an inspiring evening and performance, and we were all thrilled to have the opportunity.

Glimpse of God: Morgan and MacKenzie were inseparable growing up. God knew that the time was closing in. He gave them a chance to make another memory and a chance for MacKenzie to say good-bye.

The house construction was on schedule. We were to move in on March 3 and 4, a Wednesday and Thursday night. At the last minute the moving men had to change the plans, they would move us Thursday and Friday instead. Morgan and Meredith had scheduled to spend Friday night with my parents, but moved it to Thursday night, with the plan to stay out of school on Friday to help put things away in the new house.

That Thursday night was exhausting. Ed and I worked to the wee hours of the morning moving, carrying, and arranging. We had a couple of phone calls from the girls while at their grandparent's house, inquiring as to the progress. Their excitement was evident and contagious. They announced that they would be "home" in the late morning after they enjoyed their favorite breakfast.

Glimpse of God: My girls had a very close relationship to my parents. They spent the night that Thursday night, March 4, and had their favorite breakfast on Friday morning, waffles. In general they enjoyed being pampered by their grandparents, and in return all they needed to give was their love and attention. God allowed that good-bye. It provided a wonderful, fond memory for my parents to cling to in order to help ease their forthcoming pain.

Friday, March 5, was a day of very hard work and celebration. Ed had beautiful roses delivered in honor of the

day. The girls worked hard all
morning, putting the upstairs
of our new home in order. We
had a great day together. We
agreed on a lunch spot, and the
girls and Ed headed to the car.
Morgan and Meredith were
hungry and impatient. They
insisted that the fact that they
had to wait so long for lunch
bordered on a form of child
abuse. They sat in the car and
honked the horn . . . and of
course, the more they did that,
the longer I took getting to the
car. We teased each other
throughout lunch. Morgan was
her typical organized self and
presented us with a list of
supplies the upstairs bedrooms
and her sisters would be
needing to outfit their "dorm."
We just laughed at her. We
continued to work hard the
remainder of the day. The girls

were thrilled to finally be in the house that had consumed so much of our time and attention. What a day to celebrate!

Glimpse of God: God gave me a day and lunch with my daughters. He gave me laughter with Morgan. God knew. God saw how busy our lives had been, and He spoke to my heart and head and told me to let them miss school, which was out of character for me. I reveled in their attention, their love, and let this move be theirs, too. I listened, and I'm thankful that I did.

We ordered pizza that night, as we did nearly every Friday night, but tonight it was special. We ate in our new kitchen. Morgan was in her

robe, and Meredith was
dressed and ready to go to a
birthday party. Laughter and
kidding were alive and well in
our new home. The moving
men and Ed were at work.
Everyone had plans for the
evening, but we all looked
forward to coming home later
that night and sleeping in our
new house. Meredith was at
the party. Morgan and a
girlfriend were upstairs,
giggling and laughing about
potential prom dates. Morgan
came through the dining room
with Lindsay, announcing her
plans for the evening. I
grabbed her arm and spun her
around. There was an aura
surrounding her beautiful face
and vibrant red hair. She
glowed. As busy as I was, I
stopped and told her how
beautiful she looked. I told her

she had a glow about her. She waved me off like I was crazy, but she giggled and smiled. I asked her where she was going, what time she would be home, and then said, "I love you, Morgan, and be careful." That was the last time I saw Morgan the way I want and need to remember her.

Glimpse of God: Thank you, God, for my wonderful good-bye. Thank you for letting me say all that was in my heart. Overwhelmed by her beauty and her glow, I said all I could say—that I loved her and that she was beautiful. Parents of teenagers know that there are times they anger us. It could've been one of those good-byes. But God is a kind and loving God, and He knew what guilt I would've had to overcome, as well as pain, if it hadn't been a sweet good-bye. Thank you!

At 9:30 p.m., March 5, Morgan called. I told her that we were still carrying boxes, furniture, and belongings of all shapes and sizes into the house. She said that she and her friends had been hanging out taking pictures and just messing around. She wanted to know if she could leave and take Catherine home before she came home. She would be home close to 10 p.m. Meredith was home from her party and had changed into her pajamas. The phone rang at 9:50 p.m. We were on the porch and missed the call. Meredith suggested we use the *69 technology and find out where the call originated. We did so, wrote down the number on the only available paper, the floor covering. We realized it was MacKenzie calling from the

Washington, D.C., area where her cast was performing. My thought was, "How strange . . . she only calls on Sundays. I wonder why she called tonight?" I attempted to return the call, but received a busy signal.

Glimpse of God: MacKenzie said in retrospect that she had a overwhelming feeling to call home, that she needed to. As it turned out, that call at that minute and my record of the number on the floor paper allowed me to locate her the next morning. MacKenzie, as the oldest, was my strength. When she left to perform and travel, I had given up one of my partners and Morgan had stepped into that role. Thank you, God. Your timing is impeccable. You are an awesome God. You know what we all need.

At 10:10 p.m., March 5, 1999, my world really did stop. It crashed. It lost all sense of balance. A mother's greatest fear in this world is a telephone call telling her that there has been an accident. It weakened my knees and sickened my stomach. I felt as if a sledgehammer hit me in my head and a knife cut open my chest simultaneously. The state highway patrol dispatcher was on the phone asking where we lived. Why did he get to ask all the questions, and how dare he not answer my questions about Morgan's well-being?! The dispatcher needed to locate us. We were not where Morgan's license and vehicle registration had placed us because we had moved that very day. The dispatcher said he was sending two highway patrol men, but he had no answers to my begging to know how Morgan was or where Morgan was. How could this drama be happening in my kitchen, in front of my baby girl, Meredith? I wanted to scream; I did scream. I needed to hold my Morgan. Where was she? More important, God, where were You? Where are You? How can You hurt me like this? I'll do anything. Please be with Morgan and take care of her.

The following hours consisted of a terrifying ride to the hospital in a speeding patrol car, meeting with physicians, waiting, praying, begging, trying to listen and comprehend the details of the accident and the injuries. Screaming, crying, pushing, shoving, hitting, hoping, and, again, praying.

Three physicians came to me, two with tears in their eyes, and explained that the trauma to Morgan's head had caused brain swelling. Her brain was continuing to swell, and she showed no signs of brain activity. If, by a miracle she lived, she would be paralyzed from her neck down, but in their opinion, she would not live. I needed a second opinion . . . for me, my family, and Morgan. I needed time to pray and ask for a miracle. I needed time to digest this. The second opinion team would be to the hospital by 7 A.M. Morgan would be monitored for the next seven hours until they could be contacted and arrive.

At 5 A.M. we took Meredith home to rest. During those two hours I called the hospital twice. I paced around my cluttered home filled with unpacked boxes like a caged and angry mother lion. I needed MacKenzie. I remembered the number recorded on the floor covering. I called that number and let it ring and ring. Finally the host family answered and I explained the emergency. MacKenzie was scared. I told her it was bad. I told her I needed her to come home now. I called one of Morgan's teachers who was also a travel agent to arrange for MacKenzie to come home. She handled all the rest.

Glimpse of God: Thank you, Lord, for all of the friends we have made. Thank you for the children and their ability to work well with their teachers and develop relationships with them. Thank you for bringing MacKenzie home safely to me. God worked several amazing miracles that night, but not the one I prayed for. God has His own agenda. Faith is being able to accept His agenda when it does not match yours.

The accident itself was a freak series of events. Morgan was driving her red Jeep west on Young's Road at 45 mph. The moon was full and orange. It was her favorite road because it is full of horse farms and she loved to ride in that area. Morgan was buckled in her seatbelt, as were her three friends and

passengers. The heat of the car was on high and she got hot. She wanted to remove her coat. Morgan unbuckled her seatbelt, removed her coat, and never refastened her seatbelt. In the next thirty seconds or less, she reached to change the radio station, the Jeep drifted to the right, the right tires left the pavement at a point where the pavement had built up over the years and was six to eight inches high. Morgan tried to pull the car to the left and lost control. The Jeep rolled, and Morgan was thrown from the vehicle. The other three girls were unscathed.

Upon returning to the hospital and seeing Morgan inverted to help her blood circulation, I realized that she was not there. Her spirit was all around us, but she was not in that shell of a body any longer. After hearing the second opinion, which matched the first, we knew that it was time to say our final good-byes. When our nurse asked about organ donation, we never hesitated. Why should we? Morgan had told us just weeks before, in no uncertain terms, what she wanted. Family and friends could not fathom the quickness of our decision, but Morgan had done this for us. We asked our nurse to arrange for an organ procurement representative to meet with us promptly. Less than an hour later, we were introduced to a kind, gentle individual who was full of empathy and compassion. She asked if we knew anything about the organ donation program and its importance. We explained what we knew and told her that Morgan had marked her drivers license to donate and about our conversation with her, about this subject, two weeks prior. There was no hesitation on our part. The proper papers were signed while the tears burned our eyes and cheeks. There was never any pressure to hurry our decision. The option to change our minds was availed to us up until the moment the surgery started. Morgan and I were sure of this decision. My only thought of trepidation was, "Is it fair that God take one life in order for another to have a chance to live?"

Glimpse of God: In God's arrangement, we all have a time for joy and a time for tears. In the Holy Master's scheme, our days are numbered. When it is time for happiness, enjoy and be thankful, for tomorrow's joy is for another and sorrow is for us. Thank you, God, for having a balance, for in that balance we find depth and we grow. Thank you for helping me through our loss to learn to laugh and cry with others more easily.

The organ procurement agency in our area is the Carolina Donor Services. The program is invaluable. The hospital representative, surgeons, and the follow-up staff are empathetic individuals that know and share your pain. Our daughter was able to share her life with others that she would never know. Organ donation is a gift that one can give to others. It is one of the most worthwhile endeavors in human kindness. There is no cost to the donating family. There is no pressure. There is only the hope that with donation of organs, up to fifty people can have the gift of life or their quality of life will be improved dramatically. It does not mean Morgan will live on through others . . . she simply gave the gift of life. Morgan will live on in our hearts forever.

By now, the waiting room was full. The word had spread. Everyone wanted to see Morgan. Everyone wanted to console, talk, or hug. I wanted to go home, and we did.

The darkness. Oh, you hear about it. You read about it. But what do they mean, darkness? It is real. It is a black tunnel. I know it was my body's way of protecting me, to shelter me. It was as frightening to me as the events that brought it. It was shock. Regardless, it was another of the surprising events that pain places in front of you.

MacKenzie arrived home at 1:30 p.m. on March 6. By then the house was full of people, and still the miserable boxes were everywhere. Flowers were arriving. One woman delivered roses in tears. She had just delivered "celebration roses" the day before on one of the happiest days of our lives. Now she delivered condolence roses on the saddest day of our lives. Ed and friends started moving boxes onto the porch to allow more room in the house. I needed to run away. MacKenzie came out on the porch with me. I wailed like a bawling calf for its mother. I told her I wanted just fifteen minutes with Morgan and that I needed to be with her. I wanted to take those minutes and make sure she knew how much I loved her and hear her tell me how much she loved me. I wanted to go be with her!

This was the first of many suicidal thoughts I had. MacKenzie said that I could not have that time with Morgan and that I couldn't leave my other daughters, so please don't even think it. She said that I would get an answer from Morgan, but not in the way I imagined. It

would not be a conversation
with her, but something would
surface and show me an
answer to my needs. I cried. I
did not want to be on this earth
without Morgan. We were a
matched set of buttons and
now one was missing. . . and
now all the buttons would
have to change.

We started emptying boxes
to put our energy to good use.
I reached down and handed
MacKenzie some kitchen items.
Something caught my eye. A
piece of white paper stuck
between some box flaps. I
pulled it out and found that it
was last year's Mother's Day
card from Morgan. She was
artistic and always made me
cards. It read," Thank you for
loving me Mom, I love you
back a whole lot." That was
what I needed. That was my

fifteen minutes with Morgan
that calmed my many doubts
and fears.

*Glimpse of God: God granted me
the finishing of our home.
Morgan's graduation into heaven
would be honored by many, and it
was. He knew we would need the
room, for the house we had lived
in and rented for the past six
months was tiny. God came when
I needed Him. At the moment of
desperation on the porch, He gave
me the card with the answers I
needed. God is always there when
you need Him most. He works on
His timetable and He decides
when it is beyond our being able
to handle it.*

On March 8, a memorial
service was held at Morgan's
"growing up" church. Both of
her ministers conducted the
service. The church
overflowed. School was
dismissed early. Adults and
children came to pay tribute
and mourn the loss of a
beautiful, smart young woman.
The students from Morgan's
Advanced Placement art class
handled all the details of the
service, from the candlelight
vigil and the high school
choir's singing to the display
of Morgan's artwork in the
narthex. Over 500 people
attended to say good-bye.

A second memorial service
was held for the scattering of
Morgan's remains. It was
planned by her art teacher and
classmates. Her teacher knew

how much Irish meant to Morgan. She knew that Irish needed closure as much as we did. The British Horse Society service took place with Irish scattering Morgan's ashes on one of her favorite riding areas, the Moss Foundation in Southern Pines. A stone marks her resting place and signifies her love of the horse and the jump.

Glimpse of God: God heard my prayers. I gave it to Him. The questions of what to do with Morgan's remains nagged at me. I prayed. That very morning of my prayer, a call came in suggesting this type of ceremony. I said yes! Thank you God for listening and helping with these plans at a time when I could not handle anything else.

I will interject here some additional insight into Morgan and her unique personality, relationships, and work ethic. Morgan held two jobs. She worked from the time she was fourteen years old. She planned everything and every day. Because she worked, she developed relationships with the adult community as well as with her peers. She wanted to be successful in the field of art and had a master plan to pursue it as a career. Morgan liked to joke around. She liked everyone and always tried to be kind. She knew what it was like to be an outcast—her red hair and freckles attributed to her empathy for people because she suffered a great deal of harassment in her younger years. Morgan was bright and shiny. She was a silent leader and refused to deface and degrade herself by partying with her friends. Morgan had high standards and values, and her goal was to bring others up to her level through encouragement. She achieved this often. Morgan was well liked and popular, but most of all, she was consistent.

March 13–March 23

Time passed so quickly, and yet the days were long and sleepless. I became very predatory about the mail and the condolence cards. I saved them to open at 11:30 to midnight each night. I read every line of every card. My family thought it was very unhealthy. I would look for one word or one line that would sustain me until the next night. I wanted to know that God was with me, but I kept thinking that all the events that were taking place were not His gifts. Rather, coincidence or fate—anything but this God who had allowed this to happen. How dare He barge in and take away my hopes for the future in Morgan? He was cruel, and I was saddened.

The assistant pastor from our church visited me at our home on March 23. We talked, but mostly we prayed and asked God to present someone to come into my life that has experienced a very similar loss. I was suicidal. I did not know how to do this alone. I wasn't alone. God was there for me, but I did not know what to think, feel, or expect. I needed

someone who had lost a
teenager. I needed someone
who had enjoyed their child
and had gotten to know their
child like I had.

By April 7 I was still feeling
quite desperate. If I left this
world, MacKenzie and
Meredith would suffer even
more. I felt so torn and
confused. I wanted to see the
"good" or "light" in this
tragedy, but where was it?

Dr. Goodwin, Morgan's
orthodontist asked if he could
have someone call me,
someone who might be able to
help. I agreed. On April 13 I
gave a speech and awarded a
National Honor Society
scholarship in Morgan's honor.
After the induction and speech,
we went to get ice cream. I told
Ed that the tunnel, the

darkness was returning, and I was falling in deeper this time. I felt more desperate than ever.

That very night at 10 p.m. the phone rang and the voice at the other end of the line sounded like an angel. She did not know it, but she saved my life. She called on Dr. Goodwin's recommendation. Her name was Allison McLean. She had lost a child, a teenager, nine months ago. Her son, Chris, like Morgan, was a good boy. He was centered, smart, enthusiastic, well liked, and well rounded—the description was that of a male version of Morgan. Chris was killed in a Jeep accident, on a Wednesday night, and died of the same head trauma that had taken Morgan's life. Allison asked me to meet her, and she would share with me her journey through this darkness. She would share with me how she survived. She would tell me about her "faith journey" since her loss.

Two days later I met Allison for lunch in her hometown. The bond was there and we quickly developed a friendship that I know will last a lifetime. She came prepared. She provided me with paper, pencil, a journal book, and a list of scriptures that would provide strength. She gave me tapes and made me take notes. She even gave me homework. Most of all she gave me *life* and *hope*.

Glimpse of God: Thank you, God, Morgan, and Chris, for orchestrating the meeting of two mothers that would eventually help one another. Thank you for answering yet another of my prayers. God, in your divine wisdom, thank you for giving me Allison, this angel of hope. God puts people in our path for reasons unknown. Thank you, God, for putting she and I together on this path which we presently wander.

April 17–May 1

I worked very hard to learn God's word and works. I started journaling all the previous days, creating a true account of what had happened. I did not ever want to forget. I was afraid as I grew old and gray and feeble in my mind that I might forget her. I wanted to remember it all. Morgan was worth all of that. Most important, though, as I started recollecting all the events, I saw a pattern of God being with me. He was there each time I needed Him. He never abandoned me. In writing in my journal and reliving the days since the accident. I began to open my eyes and my heart, enabling me to see and feel the glimpses of God. It was His way of talking to me.

Despite my "homework," on May 3, I hit another low point. It was a Monday morning. I was on a conference call with work and in my periphery were two beautiful pictures of Morgan that were waiting to be hung in the upstairs hallway. As the call

came to an end I could feel the
sadness and despair welling up
inside of me. I cried hyster-
ically as my mind whirled with
all of my unanswered
questions. What if all that had
happened was mere
coincidence? What if I was
desperate for divine
intervention and so I took these
everyday events and imagined
a deeper meaning? What if
there is no afterlife? What if
Morgan is just gone, and I
never see her again? I crashed.
I cried and convulsed. Ed put
me to bed and worried about
my ever being "normal" again.
Would I ever be the same? I
liked what I had accomplished
in my life and the person I was
just before the accident. How
could I survive being different
than I was for the past forty-
five years? It was the only day

I stayed in bed, but it was nearly two months since the accident. Shouldn't I be getting better? I prayed in my bed. I asked God to give me answers. I asked Him to love me and take care of me and to help me understand suffering and why I have to suffer.

I decided the next morning that I needed to get back on track. During the previous two months I had worked the entire time. There wasn't room for breakdowns like the one the day before if I wanted to keep my job. I hopped in the car bright and early and headed for Troy, about an hour or so from my home. As I got in my car I saw a tape on the dashboard of my car, a tape that Allison had given me. Oh, I hate religious tapes. As I

stated before, I barely
understand the language of the
Bible; it seems too flowery and
complicated for my shallow
mind. But I put the tape in
anyway. Sometimes the radio
or a tape can be playing, but it
provides only background
noise as you drive. You say you
are going to listen, and you do,
but very minimally. This time I
listened.

David Moore, a pastor of a
California Methodist Church,
was giving a sermon. It was
based on the death of a youth
group leader in their church.
He broke down his lesson in
two areas, God's promises and
why there is suffering. I
listened more intently to his
words than I had listened to
anything in a long time. I
literally pulled off the road and
took notes several times. As he

preached he suggested a book, something he had never done in thirteen years in the ministry. He stated that the book may be difficult to find and would challenge even the smartest readers, but he felt it was important to read. The title of the book was *Disappointment with God*. I continued working that day, thinking as I drove of the things that David Moore had preached about.

That afternoon I stopped at two large bookstores and asked for the book. I was told that it was out of print. After running several errands I was returning to my car to go home when I remembered that my friend Robin had asked me to do a favor for her several weeks before. In my self-pity and self-indulgence I had neglected her

request. I did it now. I stopped
by her shop to tell her about
what I had found and to
apologize for having taken so
long to get back to her.

As I entered her shop,
Robin seemed truly glad to see
me and stopped what she was
doing to greet me. We spoke
only briefly before she touched
my arm and asked me to walk
out to her car with her. That
very morning, she said, the
strangest feeling had come
over her. While straightening a
shelf she had come across an
old book, one that she had
never read and in fact did not
even remember how she came
to have it. She was planning to
throw it away but instead put
it in the car with her. She was
not sure if I would get
anything out of the book. She

placed in my hands *Disappointment with God*, the very book David Moore had referred to on the tape and the one I had tried to find. I cried like a baby as I related to my friend what had just taken place.

Glimpse of God: God was all around me. He was holding me up. He was hurting with me and trying to show me that He was with me and would never let me down. This event was beyond chance or coincidence. God was yelling at me to see His presence. It was in this event, combined with all the others, that I realized how much God loves all of us. I was humbled to think that in the vast world and the tiny speck that I am, God listens to me and my needs.

Then I was aware. I had awakened. I knew that even though He allowed my middle daughter to die on this earth, the one child that was most like me, He gave to me the ability and perception to see His greatness and journal His greatness as a layperson. Someone so common, yet someone who would not be afraid to stand in testament of Him. A new disciple with a voice that many listen to.

It was May, and everyone was abuzz over the upcoming prom. Truth be known, I hated the weeks prior to the one event that Morgan really wanted to attend. She knew she was asking one of the young men from the private school. I was jealous and envious of all the excitement. These were the very emotions that I had warned my girls against. While going through some of the remaining boxes in our storage building, I found one that was labeled "Morgan's stuff." It appeared to be empty. I tossed it aside, only to hear it thump. I looked inside and flat against the bottom was a notebook. I pulled it out and opened it. It was titled *A Book about Morgan.* She had made it for a class two years ago. It contained pictures and important events as well as a list of all of her favorites. I stood there and hugged it and felt so lucky to have this book. Most parents do not know their children's favorite anythings.

The next day I received a call from the junior class advisor. They were dedicating

the prom to Morgan and
wanted to know if I could tell
her Morgan's favorite quotes
for the program. Yes! I knew
her favorite quotes and went
on to explain the miracle in
finding this notebook prior to
this request.

*Glimpse of God: God knew that I
would be asked for Morgan's
favorite quotes. He handed them
to me to ease any stress and pain
that I might have to endure
looking for her favorites. God
knows everything before it
happens. His plan leaves nothing
to chance. Thank you for giving
her "favorites" to me so that I
could share them with so many.*

By mid-May I was getting
scared. I was forgetting
Morgan's voice and her

mannerisms. I needed to hear her voice. I wanted to remember and capture everything. Damn it! We had never had a video camera. I went by the school to deliver something and saw Morgan's art teacher and friend. She asked how I was doing and mentioned that she came across the videos of the debates from art class. She offered them to me. Wow!

Glimpse of God: You amaze me. My wish is your command. I thought it was the other way around. God does not want me to know fear. Fear is of the enemy. I could hear Him gently whisper, "do not let your hearts be troubled and do not be afraid. . . I am here." God wants me to learn to trust in Him and ask Him. Thank you.

I finished out the month by making sure the memorial gardens created in Morgan's honor were in place. The community felt a sense of loss almost as great as my own and the outpouring of support from family and friends was overwhelming. We decided to erect five garden spots at local churches and the high school. It took a good deal of thought and planning to distribute the funds wisely and equally. I am proud that there are five beautiful reminders of Morgan's short life on earth located throughout our town.

June–August

I decided to start a business in memory of Morgan and her creative and artistic spirit. MacKenzie wanted to return to Southern Pines when her year of traveling with Up With People was complete. She agreed that starting this business would be a fun, fitting tribute and an asset to our town, which had supported our family in so many ways for years. The 9th of September, a paint-your-own-pottery studio, opened on August 10. The name is Morgan's birthday, as MacKenzie says,

"The day a great deal of creativity was unleashed on the world."

Everything fell into place for the successful opening of the business. It was easy and I knew in my heart that there

was divine intervention—
nothing could fall into place so
nicely without real help.

Putting the final touches on
the store, I climbed up a very
tall ladder to paint huge,
beautiful hearts at the
beginning and end of a quote
that was one of Morgan's
favorites. It was a 90-degree
afternoon and we had no air
conditioning yet. It was hot. I
was exhausted. Morgan and
thoughts of her overwhelmed
me. She was in my throat, and
my heart was breaking again.
These huge whimsical hearts
were for her. I had a difficult
time finishing them.

Later that afternoon I got
home just as the phone rang. I
answered, and the woman
identified herself as the
recipient of Morgan's heart.
She had been afraid to call. She

was so humbled, so thankful
for the gift we had given her.
We visited for a long time. She
is a thankful, gracious lady.
The following week I heard
from the recipients of Morgan's
liver, her pancreas, and her
kidneys. We all still
communicate.

*Glimpse of God: I know Your
miracles are different than my
requests. You know the whole
plan, the tapestry. If I knew the
plan, what kind of a God would
You be? Just ordinary, not the
awesome, all-knowing being that
You are. You performed a miracle
the night of Morgan's accident,
but not the one I requested. And
You worked so hard the following
days when You gave life to four
people and sight to one. Thank
you for having a plan and not*

*letting her life and our loss be for
nothing.*

We had been moving at a
speed that would rival the
speed of light. The
funeral/memorial service, the
gardens, starting a new
business, helping with a big
United Way fundraiser that the
store sponsored and chairing a
fundraiser for Meredith's
school, as well as running a
household and working a job. I
was weary. I had run from my
grief by frantic movement, by
filling every possible minute,
so I wouldn't feel the void and
the pain.

On October 6, Mackenzie
and Meredith asked if I would
let Meredith out of school early
so they could go to lunch and
go to the mall to shop.

Reluctantly, I agreed. The last time I let anyone miss school was in March. The girls had a good afternoon and returned bearing gifts and stories. Morgan had been the gift planner and giver, she was the sensitive one, who always came home from shopping with a trinket for Mom. Not these two. So when they came home and announced they had a surprise for me, I was shocked to find that they had purchased a beautiful shirt, just for me. They told me the story.

On the way to Fayetteville, a "moon-doggie" (a rainbow ball) followed them to the mall. While at the mall they met a clerk who reminded them of Morgan. While shopping at her store they both got an incredible feeling that they should buy me something and picked out the same thing at the same time. Then when they drove all the way home with a moon-doggie following them again, they were both sure Morgan was with them while they had a sisters' day out. I cried. That night Morgan visited me!

Glimpse of God: God gives you what you need on His schedule! He works through the hearts of many. That day God was working by laying thoughts on my children's hearts. He was conveying a peace to me that can only come through acceptance and trust. God was helping me to stop wanting what I had in my life and accept His love. Thank you for helping me to accept my situation and know that I belong to you, Lord.

I had been desperate for a dream of Morgan. Finally it came. It was twilight in the dream, that moment before you really go to sleep. She was dead in her visit with me, and we both referred to this. She said she was OK, then she showed me an awesome hay field, so lush and green. Again she told me she was OK. I asked her if the field was the farm in Ohio and she laughed so hard. She put her arm around me and very patron- izingly said, "Come on, Mom, this is way bigger that any farm in Ohio." I awoke at peace, but for the next six days the yearning to hold her, to hear her more, to see her again, nearly drove me crazy.

The months of October and November were whirlwinds. We survived two more

holidays without Morgan.
Halloween was harder than
Thanksgiving. Ed had some
great memories of Morgan
during state fair time and
Halloween. The peaks and
valleys still appeared. One
minute I could say in complete
honesty that I was doing pretty
well, and the next minute,
hour, or day, I'd bottom out.
The emotional roller coaster is
not something you can prepare
for. It defies any logic. I have
not taken any antidepressants;
a voice inside told me not to.
Instead I work at remembering
every part of what goes on
around me, in my mind and in
my heart. In all of this struggle
I have learned to listen, even if
I don't know exactly what I am
listening for.

I am happy with all that I did with Morgan. My happiness ends because she is not with me on this earth any longer, and I feel short-changed. But if I put on my hat that reads "Eternal Perspective," then I relieve myself of some of the sadness. It's hard to give up the earthly perspective, so I still work on that every day. I suffer for four reasons:

1. So I can learn to comfort others, which is why I have written all of this down.

2. So I can learn to rely on God. *The Glimpses of God* that I have journaled are a testament to my learning to rely on God.

3. So I can learn to pray for others. *The Bible* says that praying is something all of us need to work on. We should pray for the greater good first and slowly bring the prayers into our personal realm. I struggle with this because I am human and self-centered and I pray for me and my

loved ones first, but I am a student still working on this aspect of prayer.

4. So I can learn to live thankfully. At the beginning I wrote that I gave thanks to God for His many blessings and that there is a difference between being thankful and THANKFUL. Today I am THANKFUL from my toes and from the bottom of my broken heart for the small gifts God has given me.

December

I knew it would be a year of firsts. My first Mother's Day without Morgan, my first Easter, Halloween, and Thanksgiving, but nothing could prepare me for my birthday and the Christmas holiday season without one of my girls. It is funny. We do not remember what Morgan was doing on any ordinary day, but we certainly remember what she did or said on every holiday for seventeen years. That is why special days are so hard.

My birthday on December 9, 1998, was difficult because MacKenzie was in Europe. Yet Morgan and Meredith made it wonderful. They had planned a surprise birthday party at my aunt's house and pulled it off. I was shocked and overjoyed.

This year I knew I would miss Morgan, and I did. The depression hung on from the first until the fifteenth. I felt flush and dizzy almost all the time. Christmas songs tug at your heartstrings with their simple beauty. Morgan was a Christmas bug. She baked, shopped for gifts, wrapped and hid them. She was very particular about the decorating of the tree. She was missed.

The Christmas Eve service loomed ahead and I dreaded it.

On Sunday, the nineteenth, our family was to light the advent candle of love and explain how God's love comes like a light into your darkness. Now I know it does, and I live it. I became very nervous to talk of it in front of 500 people. I was still a student of this great love and light. I broke down minimally during the presentation, but by the end of the service I could not camouflage the pain, sorrow, and loss. I broke down and had to leave the church. Ashamed and sorry for drawing attention away from the beautiful service, I prayed for strength. The Christmas Eve service was a breeze.

Glimpse of God: Thank you for giving me a big heart and the ability to cry. Sometimes it comes out of left field, but You are shining in another manner through me and touching many. With you God, I am struck down, but not destroyed. I know that my weakness opens me to your grace and your power.

Our family is steeped with tradition. One that bothered Meredith was to be the only one in the Christmas morning "stairwell picture." The twins were with their mother, and MacKenzie was with her fiancée's family; that left just Meredith. Christmas morning we woke to an inch of snow, sticking to everything. A white Christmas! We hopped out of bed and woke Meredith; she threw all caution to the wind,

bounding down the stairs and
out the door in just her
pajamas, camera in hand, to
get pictures. When she came
in, she and I sat on the stairs
for a "stair picture" and the
gift-opening festivities started.
Later we found out it snowed
in very limited locations:
Southern Pines (our home),
Sanford (where the twins
were), and Laurinburg
(Allison's home) that morning.

*Glimpse of God: Thank you, God
and Morgan and Chris, for giving
us a diversion and not letting our
fear of the empty stair picture
dominate an already difficult
morning. Thank you for giving us
a perfect Christmas card morning.
Thanks, Christmas Bug. I find
great comfort in knowing that my
family is held in the hands of the*

One whose resources are greater than my own. Thank you for being an infinite God.

I mentioned that some of my grief was masked by constant motion, just as a firefly only shines when on the wing. So it is with me—when I stop, I darken. The only reason I have stopped long enough to share all of these events is because I am sick in bed now and I am listening. Even though stopping, listening, recollecting, and recording is painful and there are tears, I feel I have to do this.

In the aftermath of Morgan's death, I have struggled with which books to read. In one week I read ten books, looking for the answers but not really knowing the questions. I was desperate to hear from anyone who experienced even a similar loss. But mostly I needed to know where God was during all of this. I know now that He was right beside me. He was crying and hurting right along with me because He knew that I would not understand why Morgan had to leave me. Each day I thank God for giving me glimpses of Him and helping me finally see those glimpses for what they really are—opportunities to believe.

This story is full of pain and suffering. But even more than that, it is the story of how an awesome God will step into our lives if we just let Him. He had a stubborn, fast-moving subject to work with, but He is patient and kind. He is nearest to us when we need Him, and for that I am eternally grateful.

AFTERWORD

My gratitude to God, Michelle Peele and her family, and to Morgan can never be fully expressed in words. It is a feeling that only those who have experienced it can fully comprehend. To think that the loss of someone who was so special has given me life is so incredibly awesome that I can scarcely comprehend it myself. And yet I'm alive because of Morgan's unselfish desire to donate her organs. Her mother stated that the decision she had to make was easier because of Morgan's decision. I thank God every day for Morgan's gift—the blessing of life.

There are many others who are waiting for a heart or another vital organ that will save their life or give them a better quality of life. I pray that each one who reads this will consider becoming an organ donor. There is a phone number you can call to get a brochure that will answer your questions about transplants. If you decide this is something you want to do, please make your wishes known to your family and friends. Please call 1-800-355-SHARE. I have been a donor for years.

With much gratitude always,
Jessie "Harriette" Harris Riggs
Heart recipient 1999

I would like to extend an invitation to all who have read
Glimpses of God.

If you have witnessed and enjoyed any "glimpses" in
your lives, I would love for you to share them
and to hear from you.

Please write me at:

Michelle Peele
c/o Pentland Press
5122 Bur Oak Circle
Raleigh, NC 27612

or

m_peele@mindspring.com

Acknowledgments

My deepest thanks to my very close friend, Liz Brophy, who was the first to read and edit this book and stayed on-call to keep my computer up and running.

To Allison and Steve McLean for helping me through the darkest valleys and for being a continual inspiration for me.

To Louie and Pat Scribner for their support and love and for lending their ear.

To Kim Stout for her creative spirit.

To God and Morgan for watching over me, guiding me, and helping me feel their abounding love.

The sale of this book will benefit
organ donor awareness education
throughout the United States.